Introduction

Overview of the book's purpose

The purpose of this book, "The Power of Personal Branding: A Handbook for Job Seekers," is to provide guidance and strategies for individuals in various stages of their careers who are looking to enhance their personal brand. Whether you are a recent graduate, a career changer, an entrepreneur or freelancer, long-term unemployed, young professional in the creative industries, or a tech professional, this book is designed to help you build a strong personal brand that will set you apart in the competitive job market.

For recent graduates, personal branding is essential for standing out among the sea of other job applicants. This book will teach you how to showcase your unique skills, experiences, and strengths in a way that resonates with potential employers. By developing a strong personal brand, you will increase your chances of landing your dream job and kickstarting your career on the right foot.

Career changers face the challenge of rebranding themselves to fit into a new industry or role. This book will provide you with the tools and techniques to successfully transition into a new career path by leveraging your transferable skills and experiences. By crafting a compelling personal brand that highlights your adaptability and willingness to learn, you will be able to make a smooth and successful career change.

Entrepreneurs and freelancers rely on their personal brand to attract clients and build their business. This book will show you how to establish a strong online presence, create a consistent brand message, and differentiate yourself from your competitors. By mastering the art of personal branding, you will be able to attract more clients, increase your revenue, and grow your business.

For long-term unemployed individuals, personal branding can help you overcome the stigma of being out of work for an extended period. This book will teach you how to position yourself as a valuable asset to potential employers, despite your time away from the workforce. By showcasing your skills, experiences, and passion for your field, you will be able to re-enter the job market with confidence and success.

Young professionals in the creative industries and tech professionals face fierce competition in their respective fields. This book will provide you with the strategies and tactics to build a personal brand that reflects your creativity, innovation, and expertise. By establishing yourself as a thought leader in your industry, you will attract new opportunities, form valuable connections, and advance your career to new heights.

Who this book is for

Are you a recent graduate, unsure of how to stand out in a competitive job market? Are you a career changer, looking to rebrand yourself and pivot into a new industry? Perhaps you're an entrepreneur or freelancer, seeking to establish a strong personal brand to attract clients and opportunities. Or maybe you're a long-term unemployed individual, hoping to revamp your image and re-enter the workforce with confidence. Whatever your situation may be, "The Power of Personal Branding: A Handbook for Job Seekers" is the book for you.

This book is designed for individuals who understand the importance of self-branding in today's job market. Whether you're a young professional in the creative industries or a tech professional looking to make a name for yourself, this handbook will provide you with the tools and strategies needed to effectively market yourself and stand out from the crowd. Through practical tips, real-life examples, and actionable advice, you'll learn how to craft a compelling personal brand that showcases your unique skills, strengths, and experiences.

If you're feeling stuck or unsure of how to differentiate yourself in a sea of job applicants, this book will help you uncover your personal brand identity and communicate it effectively to potential employers. By understanding the power of personal branding and how it can positively impact your job search, you'll be better equipped to navigate the challenges of today's competitive job market. Whether you're looking to land your dream job, attract new clients, or simply boost your professional reputation, "The Power of Personal Branding" will provide you with the guidance and inspiration you need to succeed.

No matter where you are in your career journey, this book is a valuable resource for anyone looking to enhance their personal brand and take their professional image to the next level. Whether you're just starting out or looking to make a career transition, the strategies and insights shared in this handbook will empower you to build a strong personal brand that sets you apart from the competition. So, if you're ready to take control of your career and unlock new opportunities, "The Power of Personal Branding" is the book you've been waiting for.

Don't let your lack of self-branding knowledge hold you back from achieving your career goals. With "The Power of Personal Branding: A Handbook for Job Seekers," you'll gain the confidence and skills needed to position yourself as a top candidate in your field. Whether you're a recent graduate, a career changer, an entrepreneur, or a freelancer, this book is your roadmap to success in the world of job seeking and self-branding. So, why wait? Start building your personal brand today and watch as new doors of opportunity open for you.

How the reader can benefit from this book

In this subchapter, we will explore how readers can benefit from "The Power of Personal Branding: A Handbook for Job Seekers." Whether you are a recent graduate, career changer, entrepreneur, freelancer, long-term unemployed individual, young professional in creative industries, or a tech professional, this book is designed to provide you with the tools and strategies needed to effectively brand yourself in today's competitive job market.

First and foremost, this book will help you understand the importance of personal branding in today's job market. With more and more employers turning to social media and online platforms to vet potential candidates, it is essential to have a strong personal brand that accurately represents who you are and what you have to offer. By following the guidelines and exercises outlined in this book, you will be able to create a compelling personal brand that sets you apart from the competition.

Additionally, "The Power of Personal Branding" will help you identify your unique skills, strengths, and values, and showcase them in a way that resonates with potential employers or clients. By understanding your personal brand, you will be able to confidently communicate your value proposition in job interviews, networking events, and online platforms, increasing your chances of landing your dream job or attracting new clients.

Furthermore, this book will provide you with practical tips and strategies for building and maintaining a strong personal brand over time. From creating a professional online presence to networking effectively and leveraging social media platforms, you will learn how to consistently communicate your personal brand and stay top-of-mind with potential employers or clients.

Ultimately, "The Power of Personal Branding" is a comprehensive handbook that will empower you to take control of your career and stand out in a crowded job market. By investing in your personal brand and following the advice outlined in this book, you will be able to position yourself as a valuable and in-demand professional, no matter what stage of your career you are in.

Chapter 1: Understanding Personal Branding

What is Personal Branding?

In today's competitive job market, personal branding has become more important than ever. But what exactly is personal branding? Simply put, personal branding is the practice of marketing yourself and your career as a brand. It involves identifying and communicating your unique value proposition to potential employers, clients, and colleagues. Personal branding is all about showcasing your skills, strengths, and personality in order to stand out from the crowd and make a lasting impression.

For recent graduates, career changers, entrepreneurs, freelancers, long-term unemployed individuals, and young professionals in creative industries and tech fields, personal branding can be a powerful tool for advancing your career. By defining your personal brand, you can differentiate yourself from the competition and position yourself as an expert in your field. This can help you attract new opportunities, build a strong professional network, and ultimately achieve your career goals.

Personal branding is not just about creating a flashy resume or a catchy LinkedIn profile. It's about authentically representing who you are and what you have to offer. This means identifying your unique skills, strengths, and values, and finding ways to communicate them effectively to your target audience. Whether you're a recent graduate looking for your first job, a career changer exploring new opportunities, or a freelancer trying to attract clients, personal branding can help you showcase your expertise and make a positive impression on others.

One of the key components of personal branding is consistency. Your personal brand should be reflected in everything you do, from your resume and cover letter to your social media profiles and networking interactions. By presenting a cohesive and authentic image of yourself across all channels, you can build credibility and trust with your audience. This can help you establish yourself as a thought leader in your industry, attract new opportunities, and achieve long-term success in your career.

In the digital age, personal branding has never been more important. With the rise of social media and online networking platforms, it's easier than ever to showcase your skills and expertise to a global audience. By investing time and effort into building your personal brand, you can create new opportunities, expand your professional network, and take your career to the next level. So whether you're a recent graduate, career changer, entrepreneur, freelancer, or long-term unemployed individual, now is the time to start thinking about your personal brand and how you can leverage it to achieve your career goals.

Importance of Personal Branding for Job Seekers

In today's competitive job market, personal branding has become more important than ever for job seekers. Whether you are a recent graduate, a career changer, an entrepreneur, a freelancer, someone who has been unemployed for a while, or a young professional in the creative or tech industries, establishing a strong personal brand can set you apart from the competition and help you land your dream job.

One of the key benefits of personal branding for job seekers is that it helps you stand out in a crowded job market. With so many qualified candidates vying for the same positions, having a unique personal brand can make you more memorable to potential employers. By showcasing your skills, experience, and personality in a compelling way, you can make a lasting impression and increase your chances of getting noticed.

Furthermore, personal branding can help you build credibility and establish yourself as an expert in your field. By consistently sharing valuable content, showcasing your achievements, and highlighting your unique strengths, you can demonstrate to employers that you are a professional worth hiring. This can not only help you land job interviews but also position you as a thought leader in your industry.

Additionally, personal branding can help you network more effectively and expand your professional connections. By sharing your personal brand online through social media, blogs, and networking events, you can attract like-minded individuals and potential employers who are interested in what you have to offer. This can lead to new job opportunities, partnerships, and collaborations that can further your career goals.

In conclusion, personal branding is an essential tool for job seekers looking to differentiate themselves in a competitive job market. By establishing a strong personal brand, you can stand out, build credibility, expand your network, and increase your chances of landing your dream job. Whether you are a recent graduate, a career changer, an entrepreneur, a freelancer, someone who has been unemployed for a while, or a young professional in the creative or tech industries, investing in your personal brand can pay off in big ways for your career.

Chapter 2: Assessing Your Current Brand

Self-Reflection and Assessment

Self-reflection and assessment are crucial components of personal branding for job seekers. Before you can effectively market yourself to potential employers or clients, you must first understand who you are, what you bring to the table, and what sets you apart from the competition. This process involves taking a deep dive into your skills, experiences, values, and goals in order to create a strong personal brand that accurately represents who you are and what you have to offer.

For recent graduates, self-reflection and assessment can help you identify your unique strengths and weaknesses as you navigate the transition from student to professional. By taking the time to reflect on your academic achievements, extracurricular activities, internships, and part-time jobs, you can begin to craft a personal brand that highlights your skills and experiences in a way that is attractive to potential employers.

Career changers face a different set of challenges when it comes to self-reflection and assessment. Making the decision to switch industries or roles requires a deep understanding of your transferable skills, as well as a clear vision of your new career goals. By reflecting on your past experiences and assessing your strengths and weaknesses, you can create a personal brand that showcases your ability to adapt, learn, and thrive in a new environment.

Entrepreneurs and freelancers also benefit from self-reflection and assessment as they work to establish and grow their businesses. By taking the time to assess your strengths, weaknesses, opportunities, and threats, you can identify areas for improvement and develop a personal brand that sets you apart from the competition. This process can help you attract new clients, build credibility in your industry, and achieve long-term success as a self-employed professional.

For long-term unemployed individuals and young professionals in creative industries or tech fields, self-reflection and assessment can be a powerful tool for reigniting your career and finding new opportunities for growth. By taking stock of your skills, experiences, and accomplishments, you can create a personal brand that positions you as a valuable asset to potential employers or clients. This process can help you stand out in a competitive job market and land the opportunities you deserve.

Identifying Your Strengths and Weaknesses

Identifying Your Strengths and Weaknesses is a crucial step in personal branding for job seekers. Recent Graduates, Career Changers, Entrepreneurs and Freelancers, Long-term Unemployed, Young Professionals in Creative Industries, and Tech Professionals all can benefit from understanding what sets them apart from others in their field. By recognizing your strengths, you can highlight them in your job search and stand out to potential employers. On the other hand, identifying your weaknesses allows you to work on improving them and becoming a more well-rounded professional.

One way to identify your strengths is to reflect on past experiences and accomplishments. Think about times when you excelled at a task or received positive feedback from others. These moments can give you insight into your unique skills and abilities. Additionally, consider asking friends, family, or colleagues for feedback on what they see as your strengths. Sometimes others can see things in us that we may not recognize ourselves.

In contrast, identifying your weaknesses can be a bit more challenging. It's important to be honest with yourself about areas where you may need improvement. This could be anything from technical skills to soft skills like communication or time management. Once you've identified your weaknesses, you can take steps to address them. This might involve taking a course or seeking mentorship from someone who excels in that area.

When it comes to personal branding for job seekers, showcasing your strengths is key. You can incorporate your strengths into your resume, cover letter, and interviews to demonstrate why you are the best candidate for a position. By highlighting your unique skills and abilities, you can set yourself apart from other job seekers. Additionally, being aware of your weaknesses allows you to proactively address them during the job search process.

In conclusion, identifying your strengths and weaknesses is essential for personal branding as a job seeker. Recent Graduates, Career Changers, Entrepreneurs and Freelancers, Long-term Unemployed, Young Professionals in Creative Industries, and Tech Professionals can all benefit from taking the time to reflect on what sets them apart and where they can improve. By leveraging your strengths and addressing your weaknesses, you can position yourself as a strong candidate in the competitive job market.

Chapter 3: Defining Your Unique Value Proposition

Identifying Your Unique Skills and Qualities

In this subchapter, we will explore the importance of identifying your unique skills and qualities as a job seeker in today's competitive market. Whether you are a recent graduate, career changer, entrepreneur, freelancer, long-term unemployed individual, or a young professional in the creative or tech industries, understanding what sets you apart from the crowd is essential for building a strong personal brand.

One of the first steps in identifying your unique skills and qualities is to take an inventory of your strengths, weaknesses, interests, and values. This self-assessment will help you better understand what you bring to the table and how you can leverage those attributes in your job search. Consider what sets you apart from others in your field and what makes you uniquely qualified for the positions you are pursuing.

Next, consider seeking feedback from mentors, colleagues, or friends who know you well. They can provide valuable insights into your strengths and weaknesses, as well as offer suggestions for areas of improvement. Sometimes, we may overlook certain skills or qualities that others perceive as valuable, so getting an outside perspective can be incredibly helpful in honing your personal brand.

Once you have a better understanding of your unique skills and qualities, it's important to showcase them in your resume, cover letter, and online profiles. Highlight specific examples of how you have demonstrated these skills in past roles or projects, and tailor your messaging to align with the job opportunities you are pursuing. By effectively communicating your strengths and qualifications, you will increase your chances of standing out to potential employers.

Finally, don't be afraid to embrace your authenticity and let your personality shine through in your personal brand. Being genuine and true to yourself will not only attract the right opportunities but also help you build meaningful connections with others in your industry. Remember, your unique skills and qualities are what make you valuable as a job seeker, so don't be afraid to own them and use them to your advantage in your job search.

Crafting Your Personal Brand Statement

Crafting Your Personal Brand Statement is a crucial step in establishing your professional identity and standing out in today's competitive job market. Whether you are a recent graduate, career changer, entrepreneur, freelancer, long-term unemployed individual, or a young professional in the creative or tech industries, having a strong personal brand statement can help you effectively communicate your unique value proposition to potential employers or clients.

Your personal brand statement should be a concise and compelling summary of who you are, what you do, and what sets you apart from others in your field. It should reflect your values, strengths, skills, and goals, as well as your passion and personality. Think of it as your elevator pitch - a brief but powerful introduction that captures the essence of your personal brand and leaves a lasting impression on your audience.

To craft an effective personal brand statement, start by identifying your unique selling points and defining your target audience. What makes you stand out from the crowd? What are your core strengths and skills? Who do you want to attract with your personal brand? By answering these questions, you can create a statement that is authentic, relevant, and appealing to your desired audience.

When writing your personal brand statement, keep it clear, concise, and specific. Avoid using jargon or buzzwords that may confuse or alienate your audience. Instead, focus on highlighting your key strengths, experiences, and achievements in a way that resonates with your target audience. Use language that reflects your personality and values, and be sure to tailor your statement to suit the industry or niche you are targeting.

Finally, remember that your personal brand statement is not set in stone. As you grow and evolve in your career, you may need to adjust and refine your statement to reflect your changing goals and aspirations. Be open to feedback and willing to experiment with different versions of your statement until you find one that truly represents who you are and what you stand for. By crafting a strong personal brand statement, you can set yourself apart from the competition and position yourself for success in your chosen field.

Chapter 4: Building Your Online Presence

Optimizing Your LinkedIn Profile

In today's competitive job market, having a strong personal brand is essential for standing out from the crowd. One of the most powerful tools for showcasing your personal brand is your LinkedIn profile. In this subchapter, we will discuss strategies for optimizing your LinkedIn profile to attract potential employers, clients, and collaborators.

The first step in optimizing your LinkedIn profile is to ensure that your profile picture and headline are professional and attention-grabbing. Your profile picture should be a high-quality, recent photo of yourself in professional attire. Your headline should be a concise and compelling statement that describes who you are and what you do. For example, "Recent Marketing Graduate with a Passion for Social Media" or "Experienced Tech Professional Seeking New Opportunities."

Next, you should focus on optimizing your summary section. This is your opportunity to tell your story and showcase your unique skills and experiences. Use this section to highlight your accomplishments, goals, and passions. Be sure to include keywords related to your industry or field of expertise to make it easier for recruiters and potential clients to find you.

When it comes to your experience section, be sure to include detailed descriptions of your past roles and accomplishments. Use action verbs and quantifiable results to showcase the impact you've had in previous positions. Additionally, consider adding multimedia elements such as links to projects, articles, or videos that demonstrate your skills and expertise.

Finally, don't forget to engage with your network on LinkedIn. Connect with colleagues, mentors, and industry influencers, and participate in relevant groups and discussions. By engaging with others on the platform, you can increase your visibility and credibility, and potentially uncover new opportunities for collaboration or employment. Remember, your LinkedIn profile is not just a digital resume – it is a powerful tool for showcasing your personal brand and connecting with others in your industry. By following these strategies for optimizing your profile, you can maximize your chances of success in today's competitive job market.

Creating a Personal Branding Website

Creating a personal branding website is an essential step for anyone looking to stand out in today's competitive job market. Whether you are a recent graduate, career changer, entrepreneur, freelancer, long-term unemployed individual, or a young professional in the creative or tech industries, having a strong online presence can make all the difference in landing your dream job or attracting clients to your business.

The first step in creating a personal branding website is to choose a domain name that reflects your personal brand. This could be your name, a tagline that represents your unique selling point, or a combination of both. Make sure the domain name is easy to remember and reflects the image you want to portray to potential employers or clients.

Once you have selected a domain name, it's time to design your website. Choose a clean and professional layout that is easy to navigate and showcases your skills, experience, and accomplishments. Include a professional headshot, a brief bio, your resume or portfolio, and any other relevant information that will help visitors get to know you and your personal brand.

In addition to your resume and portfolio, consider adding testimonials from past clients or employers, as well as any awards or certifications you have received. This social proof can help build credibility and trust with potential employers or clients. Don't forget to include contact information so that interested parties can easily get in touch with you.

Finally, regularly update your personal branding website with new projects, achievements, or blog posts that showcase your expertise and passion for your industry. This will not only keep your website fresh and engaging but also demonstrate to visitors that you are actively engaged in your field. By following these steps, you can create a personal branding website that sets you apart from the competition and helps you achieve your career goals.

Chapter 5: Networking and Building Relationships

Networking Strategies for Job Seekers

Networking is a crucial aspect of any job search, and it can often make the difference between landing your dream job or missing out on a great opportunity. In this subchapter, we will discuss some effective networking strategies for job seekers that can help you expand your professional network and increase your chances of finding the right job.

One of the most important networking strategies for job seekers is to attend industry events and conferences. These events provide an excellent opportunity to meet professionals in your field, learn about the latest trends and developments, and showcase your skills and expertise. Make sure to come prepared with business cards, a polished elevator pitch, and a positive attitude. Remember, networking is not just about collecting contacts, but also about building relationships and making a lasting impression.

Another effective networking strategy for job seekers is to leverage social media platforms such as LinkedIn. Create a professional profile that highlights your skills, experience, and accomplishments, and connect with industry professionals, recruiters, and potential employers. Join relevant groups and participate in discussions, share valuable content, and engage with others in your field. Networking on social media can help you stay connected with industry trends, job opportunities, and potential mentors.

Networking events and online platforms are great ways to expand your professional network, but don't forget about the power of one-on-one networking. Reach out to former colleagues, classmates, mentors, and other professionals in your network to schedule informational interviews, coffee meetings, or networking lunches. Ask for advice, feedback, and referrals, and be open to new opportunities and connections. Personalized networking can help you build meaningful relationships, gain valuable insights, and uncover hidden job opportunities.

In conclusion, networking is an essential skill for job seekers in today's competitive job market. By attending industry events, leveraging social media, and engaging in one-on-one networking, you can expand your professional network, increase your visibility, and open up new career opportunities. Remember to be proactive, persistent, and authentic in your networking efforts, and always follow up with your contacts to maintain relationships and stay on their radar. With the right networking strategies, you can build a strong personal brand and position yourself for success in your job search.

Leveraging Social Media for Networking

In today's digital age, leveraging social media for networking is essential for anyone looking to build their personal brand and advance their career. Whether you are a recent graduate, a career changer, an entrepreneur, freelancer, long-term unemployed individual, or a young professional in the creative or tech industries, utilizing social media platforms can help you connect with like-minded individuals, potential employers, and industry influencers.

One of the key benefits of using social media for networking is the ability to showcase your personal brand and expertise to a wide audience. By consistently sharing relevant content, engaging with others in your field, and participating in industry-related conversations, you can position yourself as a thought leader and attract opportunities for collaboration, mentorship, and career advancement.

LinkedIn, the professional networking platform, is a valuable tool for job seekers looking to expand their network and access job opportunities. By optimizing your profile with a professional photo, a compelling summary, and detailed work experience, you can increase your visibility and attract recruiters and hiring managers. Additionally, joining relevant LinkedIn groups, participating in industry discussions, and reaching out to connections for informational interviews can help you establish valuable relationships and access hidden job market opportunities.

Twitter, Facebook, Instagram, and other social media platforms can also be powerful tools for expanding your network and building relationships with industry professionals. By following thought leaders, participating in Twitter chats, sharing industry news and insights, and engaging with influencers, you can increase your visibility and credibility within your field. Additionally, using hashtags, tagging relevant individuals, and participating in online events can help you connect with like-minded professionals and expand your network exponentially.

In conclusion, leveraging social media for networking is a valuable strategy for job seekers looking to build their personal brand, expand their network, and access career opportunities. By strategically using platforms like LinkedIn, Twitter, and other social media channels, you can showcase your expertise, connect with industry professionals, and position yourself for success in your job search. Remember to be authentic, consistent, and proactive in your networking efforts, and you will see the benefits of building a strong online presence that supports your career goals.

Chapter 6: Developing Your Branding Toolkit

Creating a Standout Resume

In today's competitive job market, having a standout resume is essential for catching the attention of potential employers. Your resume is often the first impression you make on a hiring manager, so it's important to make sure it effectively communicates your skills, experience, and personal brand. In this subchapter, we will discuss the key elements of creating a standout resume that will help you stand out from the crowd and land your dream job.

The first step in creating a standout resume is to clearly define your personal brand. Your personal brand is what sets you apart from other candidates and showcases your unique skills, experience, and personality. Take some time to identify your strengths, values, and goals, and incorporate them into your resume. This will help you create a cohesive and authentic personal brand that will resonate with potential employers.

Next, focus on creating a visually appealing and well-organized resume. Use a clean, professional layout and font that is easy to read. Make sure to include all relevant information, such as your contact information, work experience, education, and skills. Use bullet points to highlight your accomplishments and quantify your achievements whenever possible. Remember to tailor your resume to the specific job you are applying for, highlighting skills and experience that are most relevant to the position.

When writing the content for your resume, be sure to use strong, action-oriented language that demonstrates your accomplishments and contributions. Avoid using vague or generic language, and instead focus on specific examples of how you have added value in your previous roles. Use metrics and numbers to quantify your achievements, such as increasing sales by a certain percentage or completing a project ahead of schedule. This will help hiring managers see the tangible impact you can make in their organization.

In addition to your work experience and skills, consider including a section on your personal interests and hobbies. This can help showcase your personality and give potential employers a better sense of who you are outside of work. Make sure to keep this section professional and relevant to the job you are applying for. Finally, don't forget to proofread your resume carefully before sending it out. Typos and grammatical errors can make a negative impression on hiring managers, so take the time to ensure your resume is error-free. By following these tips, you can create a standout resume that effectively communicates your personal brand and helps you stand out in the job market.

Crafting a Compelling Cover Letter

Crafting a compelling cover letter is an essential step in the job application process. Your cover letter is your opportunity to introduce yourself to potential employers, showcase your qualifications, and make a strong impression that sets you apart from other candidates. In this subchapter, we will discuss the key elements of a successful cover letter and provide tips on how to make yours stand out.

First and foremost, your cover letter should be tailored to the specific job you are applying for. Avoid using a generic template and instead, take the time to research the company and the position. Highlight the skills and experiences that make you a good fit for the role, and explain why you are excited about the opportunity. Personalizing your cover letter shows that you are serious about the position and have taken the time to understand the company's needs.

In addition to customization, a compelling cover letter should also be concise and easy to read. Keep your letter to one page and use a clear, professional font. Use bullet points or short paragraphs to break up the text and make it easier for hiring managers to scan. Remember, your cover letter should complement your resume, not duplicate it. Focus on highlighting your key achievements and explaining how they relate to the job you are applying for.

Another important aspect of crafting a compelling cover letter is to showcase your personality and passion for the role. Use language that is positive and enthusiastic, and show your excitement about the opportunity. Avoid using cliches or buzzwords, and instead, focus on telling a compelling story about why you are the best candidate for the job. Remember, hiring managers are looking for someone who is not only qualified but also a good cultural fit for the company.

Finally, don't forget to proofread your cover letter before sending it off. Spelling and grammar errors can make a negative impression on potential employers and hurt your chances of landing an interview. Take the time to review your letter carefully, or ask a friend or family member to look it over for you. A well-written and error-free cover letter shows attention to detail and professionalism, qualities that are highly valued by employers.

In conclusion, crafting a compelling cover letter is an essential part of the job application process. By customizing your letter, keeping it concise and easy to read, showcasing your personality and passion, and proofreading carefully, you can increase your chances of standing out to potential employers and landing the job of your dreams. Remember, your cover letter is your chance to make a strong first impression, so make it count.

Chapter 7: Personal Branding in Job Interviews

Communicating Your Brand in Interviews

In today's competitive job market, it's crucial for job seekers to effectively communicate their personal brand in interviews. Your personal brand is what sets you apart from other candidates and showcases your unique skills, experiences, and values. This subchapter will provide you with tips and strategies on how to effectively communicate your brand in interviews to make a lasting impression on potential employers.

First and foremost, it's important to do your research before going into an interview. This includes researching the company, the industry, and the position you're applying for. By understanding the company's values, goals, and culture, you can tailor your personal brand to align with what the company is looking for in a candidate. This will show the interviewer that you've done your homework and are genuinely interested in the position.

When communicating your personal brand in interviews, it's important to be authentic and genuine. Don't try to be someone you're not just to impress the interviewer. Instead, focus on showcasing your true self and highlighting your unique strengths and experiences. Remember, authenticity is key when it comes to personal branding, and being genuine will help you build trust and rapport with the interviewer.

Another important aspect of communicating your brand in interviews is to be clear and concise in your communication. Avoid using jargon or technical terms that the interviewer may not understand. Instead, use simple language and concrete examples to illustrate your skills and experiences. This will help the interviewer better understand your personal brand and how you can add value to their organization.

In addition to being authentic and clear in your communication, it's also important to practice active listening during interviews. This means paying attention to the interviewer's questions, asking clarifying questions when needed, and responding thoughtfully and respectfully. By actively listening, you can better understand the interviewer's needs and concerns, and tailor your responses to address them effectively.

Finally, don't forget to follow up after the interview to reinforce your personal brand. Send a thank-you email or note expressing your gratitude for the opportunity to interview and reiterating your interest in the position. This will show the interviewer that you are professional, courteous, and genuinely interested in the job. By effectively communicating your brand in interviews, you can make a strong impression on potential employers and increase your chances of landing your dream job.

Handling Common Interview Questions

In the competitive job market of today, being prepared for common interview questions is essential for any job seeker. Whether you are a recent graduate, career changer, entrepreneur, freelancer, long-term unemployed individual, young professional in creative industries, or tech professional, knowing how to effectively answer these questions can make all the difference in landing your dream job. In this subchapter, we will discuss some of the most common interview questions and provide tips on how to best answer them to showcase your personal brand and stand out from the competition.

One of the most common interview questions you may encounter is "Tell me about yourself." This open-ended question is your opportunity to introduce yourself and highlight your strengths, skills, and experiences that are relevant to the job you are applying for. When answering this question, be sure to focus on your unique selling points and how they align with the job requirements. Avoid providing a long-winded answer and instead, keep it concise and to the point, highlighting key achievements and experiences that demonstrate your value to the employer.

Another common interview question that often trips up job seekers is "What are your strengths and weaknesses?" When answering this question, be honest about your strengths and be sure to provide specific examples to back them up. When it comes to weaknesses, it's important to be honest but also show that you are actively working to improve in those areas. Frame your weaknesses in a positive light by discussing how you are addressing them through self-improvement efforts or seeking out training opportunities.

"Where do you see yourself in five years?" is another common interview question that employers often ask to gauge your long-term career goals and aspirations. When answering this question, be sure to align your response with the company's goals and demonstrate how you see yourself growing within the organization. This shows the employer that you are committed to your career development and have a clear vision for your future.

"Can you tell me about a time when you faced a challenging situation and how you handled it?" is a behavioral interview question that requires you to provide a specific example from your past experiences. When answering this question, use the STAR method (Situation, Task, Action, Result) to structure your response, focusing on the actions you took to resolve the situation and the positive outcome that resulted from your efforts. This demonstrates your problem-solving skills and ability to handle adversity effectively.

In conclusion, being prepared for common interview questions is essential for job seekers in today's competitive job market. By practicing your responses and showcasing your personal brand through your answers, you can increase your chances of standing out and landing your dream job. Remember to tailor your responses to align with the job requirements and company culture, and always be honest and authentic in your answers. With the right preparation and mindset, you can ace any interview and make a lasting impression on potential employers.

Chapter 8: Personal Branding for Career Advancement

Building Your Brand within Your Current Job

As a recent graduate, career changer, entrepreneur, freelancer, long-term unemployed individual, or a young professional in creative industries or tech, it is essential to understand the importance of building your personal brand within your current job. Your personal brand is how you present yourself to the world and how others perceive you. By cultivating a strong personal brand within your current job, you can increase your visibility, credibility, and opportunities for career advancement.

One way to build your brand within your current job is to consistently deliver high-quality work. Whether you are working on a project, meeting a deadline, or interacting with colleagues, always strive for excellence. By consistently exceeding expectations, you will establish yourself as a reliable and competent professional, which will strengthen your personal brand within your organization.

Another important aspect of building your brand within your current job is to actively seek feedback from your supervisors, colleagues, and clients. By soliciting feedback, you demonstrate a willingness to learn and grow, which can help you identify areas for improvement and showcase your commitment to personal and professional development. Incorporating feedback into your work can also help you build stronger relationships with those around you, further enhancing your personal brand.

Networking is another key component of building your brand within your current job. Take advantage of opportunities to connect with colleagues, attend industry events, and participate in professional organizations. By expanding your network, you can increase your visibility within your organization and industry, as well as gain valuable insights and support from others. Building strong relationships with key stakeholders can also help you advance your career and open doors to new opportunities.

Lastly, it is important to showcase your unique skills, talents, and accomplishments within your current job. Whether you are a creative professional, tech expert, or entrepreneur, highlight your achievements and contributions in a way that demonstrates your value to your organization. By showcasing your strengths and expertise, you can differentiate yourself from others and position yourself as a valuable asset within your current job. Building your brand within your current job is a continuous process that requires commitment, self-awareness, and strategic planning. By focusing on delivering high-quality work, seeking feedback, networking, and showcasing your unique skills and accomplishments, you can strengthen your personal brand and increase your opportunities for career advancement. Remember, your personal brand is how you present yourself to the world, so make sure it reflects the best version of yourself.

Leveraging Your Personal Brand for Career Growth

In today's competitive job market, having a strong personal brand is essential for career growth. Whether you are a recent graduate, career changer, entrepreneur, freelancer, long-term unemployed individual, or a young professional in the creative or tech industries, leveraging your personal brand can set you apart from the competition and help you achieve your career goals. This subchapter will provide you with practical tips and strategies on how to effectively leverage your personal brand for career growth.

First and foremost, it's important to define your personal brand and identify what sets you apart from others in your field. What are your unique skills, strengths, and values? What do you want to be known for? By clearly defining your personal brand, you can effectively communicate your value to potential employers or clients. This will also help you create a consistent and cohesive brand image across all your professional platforms, such as your resume, LinkedIn profile, and personal website.

Once you have defined your personal brand, it's time to start building and promoting it. One of the most effective ways to do this is through networking. Attend industry events, join professional organizations, and connect with like-minded individuals on social media. By building a strong network of contacts, you can increase your visibility and opportunities for career advancement. Additionally, consider creating and sharing valuable content related to your field of expertise. This could be in the form of blog posts, articles, videos, or podcasts. By positioning yourself as a thought leader in your industry, you can further enhance your personal brand and attract new career opportunities.

Another important aspect of leveraging your personal brand for career growth is showcasing your accomplishments and skills. Make sure to highlight your achievements on your resume, LinkedIn profile, and other professional platforms. This will not only demonstrate your value to potential employers or clients but also help you stand out from other job seekers. Additionally, consider obtaining endorsements or testimonials from colleagues, clients, or mentors to further validate your expertise and credibility.

In conclusion, leveraging your personal brand for career growth is essential in today's competitive job market. By defining your personal brand, building a strong network, creating valuable content, and showcasing your accomplishments, you can position yourself for success and achieve your career goals. Remember, your personal brand is your most valuable asset, so invest the time and effort to cultivate it and watch your career soar to new heights.

Chapter 9: Managing Your Personal Brand Long-Term

Revisiting and Updating Your Brand

In the fast-paced world of job seeking and career development, it's important to constantly revisit and update your personal brand. Your personal brand is how you present yourself to the world, and it can make a huge difference in your job search and career success. Whether you're a recent graduate, career changer, entrepreneur, freelancer, long-term unemployed individual, young professional in a creative industry, or tech professional, updating your personal brand is crucial to staying competitive in today's job market.

One of the first steps in revisiting and updating your brand is to take a closer look at your online presence. In today's digital age, employers are increasingly turning to social media and online platforms to learn more about potential candidates. Make sure your LinkedIn profile is up to date and showcases your skills, experience, and accomplishments. Consider creating a personal website or online portfolio to showcase your work and stand out from the competition. It's also important to regularly Google yourself to see what information comes up and make sure it aligns with the image you want to project.

Another key aspect of updating your personal brand is to revisit your resume and cover letter. Make sure they are tailored to each job you apply for and highlight your most relevant skills and experience. Consider seeking feedback from a career coach or mentor to ensure your resume and cover letter are effectively communicating your value to potential employers. Additionally, consider creating a personal brand statement that succinctly communicates who you are, what you do, and what sets you apart from others in your field.

Networking is another important aspect of updating your personal brand. Attend industry events, join professional organizations, and connect with others in your field both online and offline. Building relationships with others in your industry can lead to new job opportunities, collaborations, and mentorship. Consider reaching out to former colleagues, classmates, and mentors to let them know you're actively seeking new opportunities and ask for their support and guidance.

Finally, don't forget to regularly assess and update your skills and knowledge. Take advantage of online courses, workshops, and certifications to stay current in your field and expand your skill set. Consider joining a professional development group or mastermind to stay connected with others in your industry and continue growing both personally and professionally. By regularly revisiting and updating your personal brand, you'll be better equipped to navigate the job market and achieve your career goals.

Dealing with Branding Challenges and Setbacks

In the world of personal branding, challenges and setbacks are inevitable. Whether you are a recent graduate, a career changer, an entrepreneur, a freelancer, long-term unemployed, or a young professional in the creative or tech industries, you will undoubtedly face obstacles along your personal branding journey. It's important to recognize these challenges as opportunities for growth and learning, rather than insurmountable roadblocks. In this subchapter, we will explore some common branding challenges and setbacks and provide strategies for overcoming them with resilience and determination.

One of the most common branding challenges that job seekers face is a lack of clarity and consistency in their personal brand. This can be especially difficult for recent graduates or career changers who may be exploring different industries or career paths. To address this challenge, take the time to define your unique value proposition and key strengths. Consider what sets you apart from other job seekers and how you can communicate this effectively through your resume, cover letter, and online presence. By establishing a clear and consistent personal brand, you will stand out to potential employers and increase your chances of landing your dream job.

Another common setback that job seekers face is rejection and criticism. Whether you are submitting job applications, attending interviews, or networking with industry professionals, rejection is a natural part of the job search process. Instead of letting rejection discourage you, use it as an opportunity to learn and grow. Ask for feedback from employers or mentors, reflect on your performance, and identify areas for improvement. Remember that every rejection brings you one step closer to finding the right job fit for your skills and interests.

For entrepreneurs and freelancers, branding challenges may include building a strong online presence and establishing credibility in your industry. In today's digital age, having a professional website, active social media profiles, and a robust portfolio are essential for showcasing your work and attracting clients. If you are struggling to build your online presence, consider investing in professional branding services or taking online courses in digital marketing and social media management. By continuously updating and improving your online presence, you will position yourself as a reputable and trusted professional in your field.

Long-term unemployed individuals may face unique branding challenges related to explaining gaps in their employment history and staying relevant in their industry. To address these challenges, focus on highlighting your transferable skills, volunteer work, and professional development activities during your time away from the workforce. Consider taking on freelance projects, attending industry events, or enrolling in online courses to stay current with industry trends and demonstrate your commitment to continuous learning. By proactively addressing gaps in your employment history and showcasing your skills and expertise, you will increase your chances of securing job opportunities and advancing your career.

Finally, young professionals in the creative and tech industries may encounter branding challenges related to standing out in a competitive job market and adapting to rapidly changing industry trends. To overcome these challenges, focus on developing a strong personal brand that reflects your unique talents and passions. Showcase your creativity, technical skills, and innovative ideas through your portfolio, projects, and collaborations with industry peers. Stay informed about industry developments, attend networking events, and seek feedback from mentors and colleagues to stay ahead of the curve and position yourself as a thought leader in your field. By embracing change, staying true to your personal brand, and continuously evolving your skills, you will navigate the challenges of the creative and tech industries with confidence and success.

Chapter 10: Case Studies of Successful Personal Branding

Success Stories of Job Seekers

In this subchapter, we will explore success stories of job seekers who have utilized the power of personal branding to land their dream jobs and achieve career success. These stories serve as inspiration and motivation for recent graduates, career changers, entrepreneurs and freelancers, long-term unemployed individuals, young professionals in creative industries, and tech professionals who are looking to stand out in today's competitive job market.

One success story comes from Sarah, a recent graduate who struggled to find a job in her field after completing her degree. Through personal branding, she was able to showcase her unique skills and experiences in a way that caught the attention of potential employers. By creating a strong online presence and networking with industry professionals, Sarah was able to secure a job at a top company in her desired field.

Another inspiring success story is that of Tom, a career changer who decided to pursue his passion for graphic design after working in a completely different industry for many years. Through personal branding, Tom was able to rebrand himself as a talented and creative designer, showcasing his portfolio and skills through social media and online platforms. This rebranding effort landed him a job at a design agency, where he is now thriving in his new career.

For entrepreneurs and freelancers, personal branding can be a game-changer in attracting clients and building a successful business. Take the example of Maria, a freelance writer who struggled to find consistent work until she focused on building her personal brand. By creating a professional website, showcasing her writing samples, and engaging with her target audience on social media, Maria was able to attract new clients and grow her freelance business significantly.

Even for long-term unemployed individuals, personal branding can open doors to new opportunities. John, who had been out of work for several years due to personal circumstances, used personal branding to highlight his skills and experiences in a way that emphasized his value to potential employers. Through networking and showcasing his expertise online, John was able to re-enter the workforce and secure a job that matched his qualifications and interests.

In conclusion, these success stories demonstrate the power of personal branding for job seekers across various industries and backgrounds. By defining and showcasing your unique personal brand, you can differentiate yourself from the competition, attract the right opportunities, and ultimately achieve success in your career. Whether you are a recent graduate, career changer, entrepreneur, freelancer, long-term unemployed individual, or young professional in creative industries or tech, personal branding can be the key to unlocking new possibilities and advancing your career goals.

Lessons Learned from Established Brands

In the competitive job market of today, it is crucial for job seekers to understand the power of personal branding. One way to learn how to effectively brand yourself is by studying established brands in the industry. By observing successful companies and their branding strategies, recent graduates, career changers, entrepreneurs, freelancers, long-term unemployed individuals, young professionals in creative industries, and tech professionals can gain valuable insights into how to build their own personal brand.

One important lesson that can be learned from established brands is the importance of consistency. Successful brands maintain a consistent image, message, and voice across all platforms and interactions. This consistency helps to build trust and credibility with customers, clients, and stakeholders. Job seekers can apply this lesson by ensuring that their personal brand is consistent across their resume, cover letter, social media profiles, and networking interactions.

Another lesson that can be learned from established brands is the importance of differentiation. Successful brands stand out from the competition by offering something unique and valuable to their target audience. Job seekers can apply this lesson by identifying their unique strengths, skills, and experiences, and highlighting them in their personal branding efforts. By showcasing what makes them different from other candidates, job seekers can attract the attention of potential employers and stand out in a crowded job market.

Established brands also understand the importance of storytelling in building a strong brand identity. By telling compelling stories about their products, services, and values, brands can create emotional connections with their audience and build loyalty. Job seekers can apply this lesson by crafting a compelling personal brand story that highlights their journey, values, and aspirations. By sharing their story authentically, job seekers can engage employers and create a memorable impression.

Lastly, established brands know the power of building relationships and engaging with their audience. Successful brands engage with customers, listen to feedback, and respond to inquiries in a timely and professional manner. Job seekers can apply this lesson by building relationships with industry professionals, networking with peers, and engaging with potential employers on social media. By actively participating in conversations and adding value to the community, job seekers can build a strong personal brand and increase their chances of success in their job search.

Chapter 11: Conclusion and Next Steps

Recap of Personal Branding Strategies

In this subchapter, we will provide a brief recap of the personal branding strategies discussed throughout this book. Personal branding is crucial for job seekers in today's competitive market, and by following these strategies, recent graduates, career changers, entrepreneurs, freelancers, long-term unemployed individuals, young professionals in creative industries, and tech professionals can effectively differentiate themselves from the competition.

The first step in personal branding is to define your unique value proposition. This involves identifying your strengths, skills, and passions, and determining how they align with your career goals. By understanding what sets you apart from others, you can create a compelling personal brand that resonates with potential employers or clients.

Next, it is essential to establish a strong online presence. In today's digital age, your online reputation can greatly impact your job search or business opportunities. By optimizing your LinkedIn profile, creating a professional website or blog, and engaging with your target audience on social media, you can showcase your expertise and build credibility in your industry.

Networking is another key component of personal branding. Building relationships with industry professionals, attending networking events, and seeking mentorship can help you expand your professional network and uncover new opportunities. By connecting with like-minded individuals and sharing your personal brand story, you can increase your visibility and attract potential collaborators or clients.

Lastly, consistency is key when it comes to personal branding. Your brand should be reflected in every aspect of your professional life, from your resume and cover letter to your email signature and business cards. By maintaining a consistent brand image across all channels, you can reinforce your credibility and make a lasting impression on employers or clients. By following these personal branding strategies, recent graduates, career changers, entrepreneurs, freelancers, long-term unemployed individuals, young professionals in creative industries, and tech professionals can effectively position themselves for success in today's competitive job market.

Action Plan for Implementing Your Personal Brand

Creating and implementing your personal brand is crucial in today's competitive job market. As a recent graduate, career changer, entrepreneur, freelancer, long-term unemployed individual, or young professional in creative industries or tech, it is essential to have a strong personal brand that sets you apart from the crowd. In this subchapter, we will discuss an action plan for implementing your personal brand to help you stand out and achieve your career goals.

The first step in implementing your personal brand is to define your unique value proposition. This involves identifying your strengths, skills, and experiences that make you stand out from others in your field. Take some time to reflect on what sets you apart and how you can leverage these qualities to build your personal brand.

Once you have defined your unique value proposition, the next step is to create a compelling personal brand statement. This statement should succinctly summarize who you are, what you do, and what makes you unique. Your personal brand statement will serve as the foundation for all of your branding efforts, so it is important to craft a clear and impactful message that resonates with your target audience.

After creating your personal brand statement, the next step is to develop a consistent brand identity across all of your online and offline platforms. This includes updating your resume, LinkedIn profile, website, business cards, and any other materials that potential employers or clients may see. Make sure that your branding is cohesive and professional, and that it accurately reflects your personal brand statement.

Finally, once you have established your personal brand and implemented it across all of your platforms, it is important to continuously monitor and adjust your brand as needed. Stay active on social media, engage with your audience, and seek feedback from colleagues, mentors, and industry professionals. By consistently refining and improving your personal brand, you will be able to achieve your career goals and stand out in a crowded job market.

www.ingramcontent.com/pod-product-compliance
Lightning Source LLC
Chambersburg PA
CBHW050247230526
45470CB00005B/2148